Kribensis Cichlid: The C
Info Guide *3*
  About Kribensis Cichlids *4*
    Temperament *5*
    Natural Habitat *6*
  Kribensis Care *6*
    Requirements *7*
    Water Parameters *8*
    Nitrogen Sensitivity *10*
    Diet *11*
  Kribensis – Common Species *11*
    Kribensis *12*
    Striped Kribensis *14*
  Kribensis Tank Mates *14*
    Suitable Tank Mates *16*
    Tank Mates to Avoid *17*
  Setting up a Kribensis Cichlid Tank *18*
    Equipment *19*
    Choosing a Substrate *21*
    Adding Live Plants *22*
    Cycling *24*

Breeding Kribensis Cichlids 26
   The Breeding Setup 27
   Setting up a Spawning Tank 29
   Determining Gender 30
   Conditioning Your Fish 31
   Inducing Spawning 32
   Parental Care 33

KRIBENSIS CICHLID: THE COMPLETE CARE, BREEDING, & INFO GUIDE

Kribensis Cichlids are a widely popular and colorful freshwater fish. They are considered both a Dwarf Cichlid and a great community tank fish. Like any cichlid, they are extremely interactive, but unlike other cichlids, they have a wider variety of possible tank mates.

The Kribensis Cichlid is a fish with unique personalities, so let's get into their care needs!

ABOUT KRIBENSIS CICHLIDS

- **Scientific Name: PELVICACHROMIS TAENIATUS, PULCHER**
- Temperament: Moderately Aggressive
- Care Level: Peaceful/ Nippers
- Origin: West Africa
- Common Names: Kribensis, Kribs, Purple Cichlid, Niger Cichlid, River Rainbow Cichlid, Palette Cichlid
- Lifespan: 5 years
- Size: 3-4"

TEMPERAMENT

These Cichlids are extremely peaceful and are normally used as community fish. They are rather small, reaching sizes of only three to four inches long, and are considered a dwarf cichlid.

They may nip the fins of certain fish, such as long finned plecos or angelfish.

The only problem with keeping them in a community tank is that they become extremely territorial during breeding. They are fabulous parents, which unfortunately includes a great deal of aggression. This can be avoided by keeping only one Kribensis or same sex pairs or groups.

NATURAL HABITAT

Kribs come from a few different rivers and deltas of West Africa with varying hardness, pH, and salinity levels. Some Kribs come from brackish and hard water areas while others come from soft, black water areas.

They come from slow moving waters packed with vegetation. These varying water parameters fortunately don't play a large role in keeping Kribensis Cichlids, as they have been domesticated for decades.

KRIBENSIS CARE

Here are some essential things you should know before attempting to keep Kribensis Cichlids:

REQUIREMENTS

While Kribs do require moderately large tanks, they can still be kept with other fish to create a wonderfully colorful community tank.

WATER PARAMETERS

Since Kribensis Cichlids come from a wide variety of water parameters, it may seem like a serious challenge to get them to fit your tank. However, it is not as much of a chore as it seems.

Kribs have been domesticated long enough to accept a variety of parameters, but you should try and match the parameters of the person, or store, you get your fish from.

Basic guidelines for Kribensis water parameters:

- pH: 5.0-8.0
- Temperature: 75-79°F
- Alkalinity: 5°-20° dGH

When keeping Kribs, stability is more important than ideal parameters. If your hardness is a bit off, it's better for the fish to adjust to your water, rather than have constantly changing parameters.

Changes to water hardness, pH, and temperature cause stress to your fish, which can shorten its lifespan.

Even though it would be better to find a local breeder with similar/ the same water parameters, this is not always possible. In that case, you will want to acclimate the fish to your water parameters.

Float the bag your fish came in and add in water, ¼-1/2 the amount currently in the bag every 3-5 minute. After every 3-4 additions, take out half of the water in the bag.

After removing the water 3 times, you can net out the fish and release it into the aquarium.

NITROGEN SENSITIVITY

Kribensis Cichlids, like all fish, are sensitive to ammonia, nitrite, and nitrates.

Ammonia and nitrites are extremely toxic and should not be present in the tank at all. Be sure to properly cycle your aquarium before adding Kribs, or any other fish.

Nitrates tend to be more of an issue for community aquariums, which is where Kribs are commonly kept. They build up over time in clean, properly cycled aquariums.

Failing to keep nitrates below 40ppm lowers a Kribensis's immune system and can lead to excess stress. It is extremely important to test your water, and the API freshwater master test kit is the most accurate test kit on the market, and cheapest per test.

DIET

Every fish should be fed multiple types of food per week. Kribensis Cichlids are omnivorous, which also make them a good community tank candidate, since they don't have a specialized diet.

They will accept flake and pellet food, though it is important to have some kind of sinking pellet, since they inhabit the lower level of the aquarium.

They will also eat anything else that drops to the bottom, whether it be frozen daphnia, frozen brine shrimp, algae wafers, or bloodworms.

Overfeeding your fish can lead to bloating problems and excess ammonia, nitrite, and nitrate, so it is important not to overfeed your fish. Feed your fish only what they can eat in 15-30 seconds two to three times a day.

KRIBENSIS – COMMON SPECIES

There are two main types of Kribensis commonly sold, with one much more popular than the other.

KRIBENSIS

Commons These are the most popular type of Kribensis sold, with a bold black stripe running horizontally down the middle of their body and another running along the top.

Their bodies are typically white, cream, and yellow in color with red stomachs. Their fins have magnificent colors and spots, including yellow, orange, black, blue, and purple.

The red will intensify during breeding season in females. The stronger the red coloration in the female, the more attracted to them the males will be.

- **Scientific Name:** PELVICACHROMIS PULCHER
- **Size:** 3-4"
- **pH:** 5.0-7.5
- **Temperature:** 75-80°F

STRIPED KRIBENSIS

These are a bit rarer in the hobby and tend to have a darker brown coloration. They have iridescent scales and tend to have a similar spotted orange-and-black tail fin to the "regular" Kribensis. They can have a gorgeous variation in color, with each fish being unique.

- **Scientific Name:** PELVICACHROMIS TAENIATUS
- **Size:** 3-4"
- **pH:** 5.0-7.5
- **Temperature:** 74-79F

KRIBENSIS TANK MATES

Kribensis tend to do very well with schooling fish like tetras and barbs. More options are available than those listed, but these are some of the more popular tank mates for Kribensis Cichlids:

SUITABLE TANK MATES

- Other Dwarf Cichlids
- Tiger Barbs
- Siamese Algae Eater
- Plecos
- Cherry Barbs
- Harlequin Rasboras
- **Corydoras Catfish**
- Congo Tetras

TANK MATES TO AVOID

Here are a few species you should not keep with your Kribensis:

- **Large Cichlids:** Fish that reach over 6-10" will likely view these fish as food. This applies to any fish that reach these sizes, but cichlids tend to be more aggressive
- **Other Kribensis:** When it comes to this cichlid, aggression is hit or miss depending on the personality. Some may be fine with others of their own kind, but some males may become extremely aggressive towards one another.
- **Invertebrates:** Small shrimp and crayfish may be eaten by your Kribensis. However, larger shrimp species, like Amano shrimp, and crayfish species like Dwarf Mexican Crayfish can work.
- **Bottom Dwellers:** Kribensis is a bottom dwelling cichlid and typically are fine with other bottom dwellers when provided with enough food. However, during spawning times, they will become extremely aggressive towards any and every other bottom dweller.

SETTING UP A KRIBENSIS CICHLID TANK

Looking to start keeping Kribensis? Here are some things you should know:

EQUIPMENT

- **Tank:** A 30- or 40-gallon tank is suitable for a breeding pair of Kribensis Cichlids, but a 50-gallon tank is recommended as the smallest size for a community tank. It is possible to breed them in a tank as small as 10 gallons, but they cannot live there permanently.
- **Filtration:** For smaller tanks, such as a 30 gallon, Hang on Back (H.O.B.) filters are acceptable, but canister filters can also be considered. For the larger tanks, canister filters are going to be your best option to keep the water perfectly clear and cycled. Whichever filter you choose, you will want to pick something that turns over the volume of the tank 7-10 times an hour for a tank that is not planted and 10-15 times an hour for planted tanks. This ensures there is enough flow and filtration for the tank to stay properly cycled.
- **Heater:** A heater is essential to keeping Kribensis as they require warm water. In some areas of the world, it may be warm enough to meet their temperature needs, but having a heater is still recommended. Without a heater, temperature fluctuations will occur.

- Even if the fluctuations are within the fish's temperature range, the changes will still cause stress to your fish. As previously established, stress can shorten your fish's live span and weaken the immune system. This means reducing stress should be a priority in keeping fish.
- **Lighting:** This is a personal choice, since Kribensis Cichlids have no specific lighting needs. Having a day/night cycle is important to fish, but aside from this, no other requirements must be met.

CHOOSING A SUBSTRATE

Kribensis Cichlids prefer darker colored substrate and will show their best colors on those substrates. They also prefer either small gravel or sand because they like to dig around in the substrate and make pits.

Large gravel will be too difficult for them to move around, which will diminish their amount of comfort. Small gravel substrate is better for live plants than sand, so if you plan on having plants, gravel would be an easier choice for beginner plants than sand.

However, plants can still be grown in sand with root tabs, so there isn't much of a difference.

ADDING LIVE PLANTS

While most cichlids destroy plants, Kribensis are overall considered plant safe. This allows for some astounding aquascaping opportunities.

Here is a list of undemanding, low light plants that will make your red Kribensis look even more amazing:

- Ludwigia
- Anacharis (Brazilian Water Weed)
- Pennywort
- Red Root Floaters
- **Java Fern**
- Anubias
- **Java Moss**
- Subwassertang
- Rotala
- Dwarf Sag
- Vallisneria
- Amazon Sword

In addition to plants, Kribensis Cichlids need to have some hardscape to hide in. Cichlid caves are commonly available in most pet stores and driftwood is also recommended.

There are many other commercially available fish caves that will work, or PVC can be used.

PVC isn't the most eye-pleasing decoration, so small gravel, plants, or rocks can be glued over the top for a more natural look.

You may also use terra cotta flower pots as caves. You will need to create an opening in the side and flip the flowerpot upside down. The best method is to use a circular drill bit to drill into the terra cotta.

Many breaks should be taken, and both the drill bit and pot should be dunked in water during the drilling process to prevent overheating. If you choose this method, be extremely cautious, and check out some more videos on the topic.

Multiple caves always need to be available to each Kribensis. Not only do the caves allow them to feel more secure, but it allows them to establish their own territories.

Most common tank mates like barbs and tetras won't have any interest in a cave, so aggression should not be a problem.

CYCLING

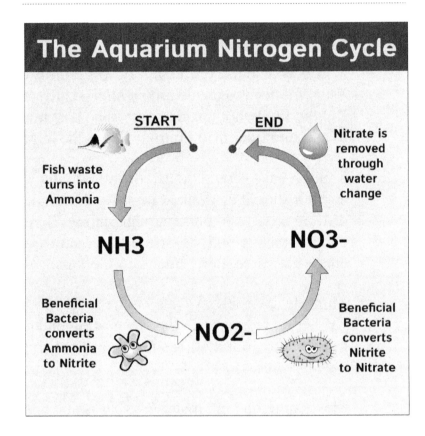

Kribensis Cichlids are extremely sensitive to ammonia and nitrite, so it is essential to cycle your aquarium before introducing any fish.

Even though you must wait to add fish, there is no need to wait to add the hardscape. This is your time to set up the aquarium exactly to your liking before adding fish.

The cycling process takes around a month, which may at first seem like a lot of wasted time, but it gives you the time to perfect your aquascape!

This also gives you time to set up your hardscape exactly how you want. Consider whether or not you want to be able to see your Kribs hiding in their caves or if you want to angle the cave openings away from the viewing area to give them more privacy.

Plants also help absorb nitrogen compounds such as ammonia, nitrite, and nitrate, and can carry in small colonies of bacteria that convert these harmful compounds to less harmful ones, so your aquascape can help in more ways than one.

This addition speeds up the cycling process, since the bacterial colonies are already established, and the only thing left to do is to build up their numbers.

For more information about cycling you aquarium, check out our fishless cycle guide.

BREEDING KRIBENSIS CICHLIDS

After keeping Kribensis Cichlids for a while, many keepers want to attempt to breed these amazing fish. Each one has their own unique personality, so it is amazing to see what kind of personalities you can produce!

THE BREEDING SETUP

Breeding Kribensis is relatively easy when compared to fish like Discus or Bettas but is more difficult than the classic livebearers.

- **Strategy #1 – Dedicated Breeding Tank:** Setting up a tank aside from the "main" or "display" tank is the first option. This includes getting a new tank, heater, and sponge filter(s) depending on the tank size. This would be necessary anyway, as the young would have to be removed before the pair spawn again. This is the more popular option when it comes to dedicated Kribensis Cichlid pairs, because those that want to breed them typically have species-only tanks.
- **Strategy #2 – Dedicated Fry Tank:** If you have a pair of Kribensis Cichlids in a community tank and want to breed them, it will be easier to set up a tank to move them to and move them back out after the eggs hatch. This tank serves as both the breeding tank and fry tank but does not serve as a permanent home. This option is typical for those that end up with an accidental pair. Be aware that they will continue to spawn unless separated and will become extremely territorial during spawning periods.

Both options are equally viable for Kribensis Cichlids and are simply a personal choice. If you don't have a community tank set up, keeping a pair of Kribs in a breeding set up would be easiest.

If you have a breeding pair in a community tank, moving them for a short period of time would be easier than moving them to a new permanent tank.

SETTING UP A SPAWNING TANK

Both options above need to be set up in the same way. Filtration should be in the form of a sponge filter to prevent fry from getting sucked up the intake of another filter and ground up in the impeller.

Unlike most breeding tanks, substrate should be present in the form of dark pea gravel or sand.

There should also be many cave options available to the Cichlids, as they spawn in the caves. They also dig holes and pits in the substrate to move fry around, which is quite an interesting process to watch.

If the tank is a dedicated breeding tank, it should be 30- to 40- gallons (or more) but if it is temporary, it can be as small as 10 gallons, though 20 is recommended.

There should also be a heater present set between 77-79 degrees Fahrenheit. Water hardness or salinity levels do not play a large role in breeding. However, the pH will determine the sex of the fry.

For pH above 7.0, you will end up with most, if not all, males, and if the pH is acidic, you will end up with females.

For this reason, most breeders try to keep their Breeding tank at a pH of 7.0 to get an even sex ratio.

DETERMINING GENDER

Kribensis males get much larger than the female, often reaching 4" in length. The females are smaller, ranging from 2.5-3". The males also have pointed tail and dorsal fins while the females have rounded fins.

Just because you have a male and females does not mean you will be able to spawn them, as this cichlid requires a bonded pair to spawn.

CONDITIONING YOUR FISH

The typical conditioning period for fish is 1-2 weeks, and the best results are achieved using live food such as daphnia, bloodworms, blackworms, white worms, fairy shrimp, and scuds.

The pair can be separated or kept together, depending on your spawning method.

INDUCING SPAWNING

Raising the temperature a few degrees, though within the range of 77-79, can help induce spawning. After conditioning, placing the pair in a new tank with multiple caves and a dark substrate and give them a few days to get comfortable.

They are not difficult to spawn and should spawn in most pH and water hardness levels, so if you give them enough time, they will eventually spawn.

PARENTAL CARE

Both parents will guard the eggs and fry for around the first month. The only responsibility on your end is to provide food for the parents and fry.

It takes around 3-8 days for the eggs to hatch and another three days for the young to finish absorbing their egg sack. While they are absorbing their egg sack, there will be no need to feed them and gives you time to set up several brine shrimp hatcheries.

Brine shrimp are a very popular fry food, and Kribensis fry are luckily large enough to be fed baby brine from the beginning.

After 1-2 weeks of feeding baby brine shrimp, some of the young should start accepting ground up flake food. Since you should also be feeding the parents at this time, some of the young may begin trying to eat some of the solid food before the 1-2 weeks are up.

If this happens, you can try and add in flake food earlier than the 2-week mark.

The best method of feeding the fry is using either a turkey baster or pipette to sneak around the parents and squirt baby brine or ground flake to the fry.

As they grow, you will have to keep careful watch of the parents' behavior. As soon as they want to spawn again, they will prioritize the survival of the next generation and may kill the previous one.

The parents do not have to stay with the fry for the entire first month, but it is very useful to have them around while the fry are still eggs.

The parents fan the eggs and eat the unfertilized eggs to protect the others from fungus. Once the fry hatch, the parents can be removed, though fry raised with the parents will end up healthier.

Whether or not the fry are sellable is based off size instead of age. Fry can be sold once they reach 1.5" and should be showing some of their coloration at 1".

They are generally worth anywhere from $3-20, with the cheaper prices occurring online where there is more competition. They are in demand, so you should have very little problem selling your fry.

Printed in Great Britain
by Amazon